starting with
STEAM

OCEAN EXPLORERS

Annette Gulati

ROurke
Educational Media
rourkeeducationalmedia.com

A Division of
Carson Dellosa Education

Before Reading: *Building Background Knowledge and Vocabulary*

Building background knowledge can help children process new information and build upon what they already know. Before reading a book, it is important to tap into what children already know about the topic. This will help them develop their vocabulary and increase their reading comprehension.

Questions and Activities to Build Background Knowledge:

1. Look at the front cover of the book and read the title. What do you think this book will be about?
2. What do you already know about this topic?
3. Take a book walk and skim the pages. Look at the table of contents, photographs, captions, and bold words. Did these text features give you any information or predictions about what you will read in this book?

Vocabulary: *Vocabulary Is Key to Reading Comprehension*

Use the following directions to prompt a conversation about each word.

- Read the vocabulary words.
- What comes to mind when you see each word?
- What do you think each word means?

Vocabulary Words:
- data
- depth
- sculptures
- study
- submarines
- technology

During Reading: *Reading for Meaning and Understanding*

To achieve deep comprehension of a book, children are encouraged to use close reading strategies. During reading, it is important to have children stop and make connections. These connections result in deeper analysis and understanding of a book.

 Close Reading a Text

During reading, have children stop and talk about the following:

- Any confusing parts
- Any unknown words
- Text to text, text to self, text to world connections
- The main idea in each chapter or heading

Encourage children to use context clues to determine the meaning of any unknown words. These strategies will help children learn to analyze the text more thoroughly as they read.

When you are finished reading this book, turn to the last page for an **After Reading Activity**.

Table of Contents

Earth's Ocean

Most of Earth is covered by an ocean. What happens under Earth's ocean?

5

Scientists that study the ocean are called oceanographers.

Scientists help us learn about the ocean.

They **study** sea animals.

They study the ocean floor.

They study the water too.

Machines and Technology

Engineers use **technology** to help scientists.

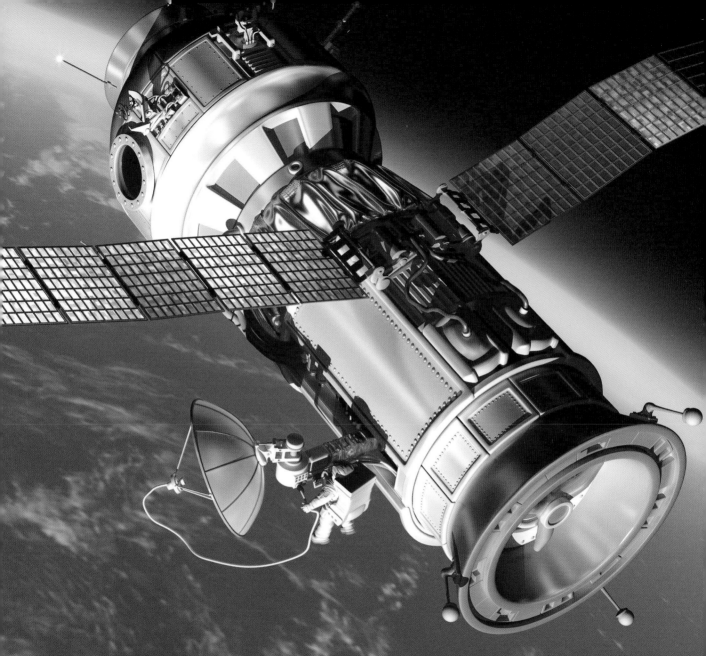

Satellites take pictures of the ocean.

Submarines help scientists explore underwater.

Robots help scientists too!

Numbers and Pictures

Scientists use math to study the ocean.

They gather **data** and make graphs.

They measure the water's **depth**.

They measure **its** temperature.

Artists use scientists' data to make **sculptures**. They draw and paint pictures of ocean life.

Many people help us learn
about Earth's ocean.

Make Your Own Submarine

A submarine can stay underwater for a long time. Test different items to see which ones make your submarine sink or float.

You will need:

- ✓ plastic bottle

- ✓ water

- ✓ marble

✓ coins

✓ ketchup packet

✓ slightly blown-up balloon

Directions:

1. Add a marble to the bottle. Fill the bottle with water. Put the lid on.

2. Put the bottle in a sink full of water. Observe what happens to the submarine.

3. Repeat with the other items, one by one.

Which item made your submarine stay midway in the water? Why? How do you think a real submarine works?

Photo Glossary

 **data** (DAY-tuh): Facts and information collected to study.

 **depth** (depth): The measurement of how deep something is.

 **sculptures** (SKUHLP-churz): Art objects shaped out of stone, wood, marble, clay, or metal.

 **study** (STUHD-ee): To spend time learning about something.

 **submarines** (SUHB-muh-reens): Ships that can travel under and on top of the water.

 **technology** (tek-NAH-luh-jee): Machines and equipment developed through science and engineering.

Index

After Reading Activity

Pretend you are a scientist. Which part of the ocean would you like to study: the sea animals, the water, the ocean floor, or something else? Draw a picture of what you might find in the ocean.

About the Author

Annette Gulati loves exploring the world and learning new things. The ocean is one of her favorite places to visit. She writes from her home in Seattle, Washington.

© 2020 Rourke Educational Media

www.rourkeeducationalmedia.com

PHOTO CREDITS: cover & title page: ©Predrag Vuckovic; table of contents: ©Christian Wheatley; p.4-5: ©Andrey Prokhorov; p.6-7, 23: ©Maravic; p.8-9: ©kanarys; p.10-11, 23: ©Konstantin Inozemtsev; p.12-13, 23: ©dstephens; p.14-15, 22: ©SolStock; p.16-17, 22: ©ADragan; p.18-19: ©darksite; p.20: ©igor170806

Edited by: Kim Thompson
Cover and interior design by: Kathy Walsh

Library of Congress PCN Data

Ocean Explorers / Annette Gulati
(Starting with STEAM)
ISBN 978-1-73161-418-6 (hard cover)(alk. paper)
ISBN 978-1-73161-213-7 (soft cover)
ISBN 978-1-73161-523-7 (e-Book)
ISBN 978-1-73161-628-9 (ePub)

Library of Congress Control Number: 2019932073

Printed in the United States of America,
North Mankato, Minnesota